82363

j761   Haddad, Helen R.
HAD
        Potato printing

82363

j761   Haddad, Helen R.
HAD
        Potato printing

DATE	BORROWER'S NAME	

POTATO
PRINTING

POTATO PRINTING

Helen R. Haddad

Thomas Y. Crowell   New York

This book is for Josette

Copyright © 1981 by Helen R. Haddad
All rights reserved. Printed in the United States of America.
No part of this book may be used or reproduced in any manner
whatsoever without written permission except in the case of
brief quotations embodied in critical articles and reviews.
For information address Thomas Y. Crowell Junior Books, 10 East 53rd Street,
New York, N.Y. 10022. Published simultaneously in Canada by
Fitzhenry & Whiteside Limited, Toronto.

Library of Congress Cataloging in Publication Data
Haddad, Helen R. Potato printing.
SUMMARY: Describes how to use an ordinary potato to
print pictures, designs, and messages on paper or fabric.
1. Potato printing—Juvenile literature.
[1. Potato printing.   2. Relief printing.   3. Handicraft]   I. Title.
TT868.H32   761   80-2458
ISBN 0-690-04088-1   ISBN 0-690-04089-X (lib. bdg.)
1   2   3   4   5   6   7   8   9   10
FIRST EDITION

Contents

Making Potato Prints 6

Potatoes and Other Things You Will Need 8

How to Print with Paint 10

Printing with a Stamp Pad 12

Lighter and Darker Prints 14

Papers for Printing 16

Monoprints 18

Geometric Printing Blocks 20

Making a Robot 22

Patterns, Letters, Butterflies, Flowers 24

Buildings and Overprinting 26

Potato Animals 28

Potato Trees 30

Trucks and Trains 32

Other Shapes for Blocks 34

Relief Prints 36

Owls and Ghosts 38

Reversal 40

Making Proofs 42

Filled-Line Prints 44

More on Filled-Line Prints 46

Carved Relief Prints 48

Using Linoleum Cutters 50

Carving with a Knife 52

Combining Blocks 54

Fabric Printing 56

Large Designs 58

Creating Backgrounds 60

Moonscape 62

Index 64

Making Potato Prints

A print is a picture made from a printing block. Instead of painting the picture directly on the paper, a printmaker makes a block, then puts the paint or ink on the block. Then the printmaker presses the block on the paper to transfer the color. The "print" is now on the paper.

Artists usually use printing blocks of linoleum, wood, or metal. But a good printing block can be made from an ordinary potato. Why potatoes? They are easy to cut and carve. They are always available. They are not expensive. Most important, they make beautiful prints.

Making potato prints is fun. You plan your picture, then you cut or carve the potato into a printing block. But you can never tell exactly how a picture made from a printing block is going to look until you print the block on paper. There is always a moment of discovery when you lift the block off the paper and see what you have made.

In printmaking you can make many, many copies of one picture or design. Potato printing blocks, like other printing blocks, can be used over and over to create new prints.

If you have never made any prints before, potatoes are perfect to begin with. If you have already done some printmaking, here are new things to try.

Each new project in this book builds on steps shown in earlier ones. Be sure to refer back for instructions.

Potatoes and Other Things You Will Need

To make potato prints, you do not need any special equipment. You will find most of your materials in the kitchen, including potatoes, knives, food coloring, cooky cutters, plates, and paper towels. You will also need paints or ink, paint brushes, and paper to print on.

You can use any variety of white potato for printing. Sometimes you will want to hunt through a bag of potatoes to find one that is a certain size or shape, but most of the time any potato will do. You do not need to peel it. However, a soft, squishy potato with sprouts sticking out all over will not make very good prints. Instead, plant it in your garden or in a flower pot where it can grow more potatoes.

A kitchen makes a good place to work. It is handy to have running water and a sink. Kitchen tables and counters make good work areas. Cover your work surface with newspaper to keep it clean and remember to put everything away when you have finished printing.

You can save your potatoes to reuse another time by putting them in a plastic bag in the refrigerator. They will keep for a week or two.

Always be careful when using knives and other sharp tools. It is a good idea to have an adult nearby while you are cutting your blocks.

How to Print with Paint

A potato cut in half makes a very simple printing block. Choose potatoes of different sizes and shapes to get different kinds of blocks.

When the block is ready, paint is spread over it. Then the block is pressed against the paper. The paint is left on the paper where the block was pressed against it, making a print the shape of the block. A printing block can be used again and again to make more prints.

Even a simple potato-shaped printing block can be used to build larger pictures. You can use one potato half or several halves of different sizes. Try arranging the potato prints on your paper so that the white spaces between the prints make a design too.

You will need: *a potato • a sharp knife • any water-base paint (poster paint, water colors, tempera) • a paint brush • paper to print on • newspaper • paper towels*

1 On a folded newspaper or cutting board, cut the potato in half with the knife. Be careful of your fingers!

2 If the potato is juicy, dry it with a paper towel. Paint the cut surface of the potato.

3 Or pour a little paint on a plate and dip the potato into it. Let extra paint drip off.

**4** Press the painted surface of the potato down on your paper. Press evenly.

**5** Pick the potato straight up from the paper. You have made a print.

**6** Apply paint again and press again. Before changing colors, wash the potato off and dry it with a paper towel.

11

Printing with a Stamp Pad

Using a stamp pad is another way to get paint onto your potato printing block. The stamp pad absorbs and holds a supply of paint. When you stamp the potato down on the pad, it picks up some of the paint. The paint comes off on the paper when you print. You can buy a stamp pad but it is very easy to make one.

You will need: *paper towels • a plate or cooky sheet • paint, food coloring, or drawing ink • a potato • a sharp knife • newspaper • paper to print on*

1 Fold a sheet of paper toweling in half and in half again. You can use a sponge or cloth in place of towels.	**2** Wet the towel. Then squeeze out most of the water. 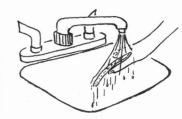	**3** Put the damp towel smoothly on an old plate, or cooky sheet. 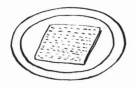
4 Pour a little ink or thin paint on the towel, or squeeze out drops of food coloring. 	**5** Try putting two or more colors on one towel. They will blend where they meet, making new colors. 	**6** If the pad gets dry, add drops of water or more paint, food coloring, or ink. Try not to get ink or food coloring on hands or clothes. It is hard to wash off.

Food coloring (the kind you use in cake icing) and drawing ink make good stamp pads. Prints made with food coloring or drawing ink—like this boat scene—have more of a water-color look than prints made using thicker paint.

1 To make a sun, sailboat, and waves: Carefully cut a potato in half. Then cut one half into halves, quarters, and eighths.

2 Look at this picture to see where you will use each cut piece.

3 Press a cut surface of the potato down on the stamp pad. Not too hard.

Now print the potato piece on your paper. Remember to lift straight up.

Lighter and Darker Prints

A potato printing block can make light or dark prints. A light print will have a soft, fuzzy look. A dark print will have a smooth, solid look.

To make lighter prints, you can print your potato block again without repainting or restamping it. Or you can thin the paint you are using by adding water. If you are using a stamp pad, you can add drops of water to the pad to lighten the color.

To make darker prints, use more paint on the potato. If you put too much, you will get a smeary print. Experiment until you find the right amount. If you are using a stamp pad, make sure there is enough food coloring, ink, or paint on the pad. Try adding a little more for darker prints.

The prints at the top of the next page were made by printing the potato block again and again without adding more color. You can see that the prints get lighter and lighter. If you want to start with a light print, you can print on scrap paper first so that most of the color will come off the block before your final print.

1 You can make a pinwheel design using an eighth of a potato half (see step 1, p. 13). First print four dark eighths.

2 Now apply the color as if you were going to make a dark print, but print two or three times on scrap paper to lighten the color.

3 Then print the block between two of the dark prints. Repeat step 2 for each light print so they will all be equally light.

Papers for Printing

Potato printing blocks can be printed on any kind of paper. But different papers, like different paints or inks, will change the look of your prints. Paint or ink sinks into some papers, such as paper tissues or newsprint. It stays on the surface of smooth, glossy papers. Watery paint or ink will always sink in (be absorbed) more than thicker paint.

Papers with raised patterns—like paper towels—will absorb the paint mainly in the raised areas, making the texture of the towel more noticeable.

Rice paper and other papers made for printing woodcuts or linocuts can be used but they are more expensive. It is interesting to experiment with printing the same potato blocks on several different kinds of paper.

Printing on colored paper will give your prints another new look. White or other light colors look well on dark colored paper.

1 To make a snowman: Pick a large round potato, a medium round potato, and a small round potato. Cut each in half.

2 Paint half of each potato thickly with white paint.

3 Now print the large piece for the bottom, the medium piece for the middle, and the small piece for the head. Use blue paper for a day picture and black for a night picture.

Draw on eyes, nose, mouth, and buttons.

  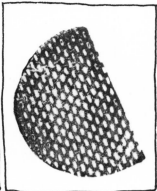 

tissue   newsprint   paper towel   glossy paper

Monoprints

To make a monoprint, you first paint a picture or design right on the potato, then print it on paper. There are two types of monoprints you can make using potato blocks, as shown below.

A monoprint is a one-of-a-kind print (from the Greek word *mono* meaning "one"). You can try making a second print from the painting on the potato, but it usually will not come out very clearly.

(Left and right sides in the painting will appear the other way around in the print. See page 40 for how to correct this "reversal.")

1 Cut a potato smoothly in half with a sharp knife. Paint a simple picture or design on it. 	**2** Gently press the potato onto your paper. Be careful not to wiggle it. 	**3** Now pick the potato straight up from the print.  Wash and dry the potato and use again.
1 To make the second type: Thickly paint the cut surface of half a potato. 	**2** Use your finger to make a design or picture in the paint. Then print gently. 	**3** Or draw in the paint using the end of a paint brush or the eraser end of a pencil. Print gently. 

Geometric Printing Blocks

Cutting potatoes into geometric shapes is easy. You can make squares, rectangles, triangles, rods, and circles. Using these shapes in different combinations, you can print animals, trains, buildings, and many simple or complicated objects.

To make straight-sided shapes, cut a potato in half on some folded newspaper or a cutting board. Then cut off the edges as shown below for the shape you are making. You can save the edge scraps and use them for printing too.

Circles are best made with circle-shaped tools.

If you want small shapes, you can cut a whole set out of one potato. For large geometric blocks use several potatoes.

You will need: *one or more potatoes • a sharp knife • newspaper • an apple corer or other circle-shaped tool*

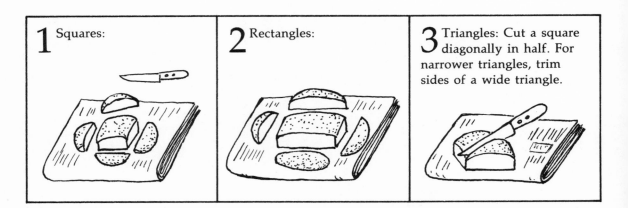

1 Squares:

2 Rectangles:

3 Triangles: Cut a square diagonally in half. For narrower triangles, trim sides of a wide triangle.

4 Rods: Cut slices off a rectangle or square.

5 Circles: For large circles, use half of a round potato, or punch down with a biscuit cutter.
For small circles, use an apple corer. Press down, then lift out.

6 For smaller circles, use the cap of a pen or a plastic drinking straw. Press in, then trim all around the cap or straw with a knife. Lift out.

Making a Robot

Only a few basic shapes are needed to make a robot. Arms and legs can be put up or down to make the robot move. You can also make people or other creatures using geometric shapes. Use circles for round heads.

You will need: *a large square • a long rod • a short rod • newspaper • paint and brush, or stamp pad • paper to print on • pen, pencil, or crayon*

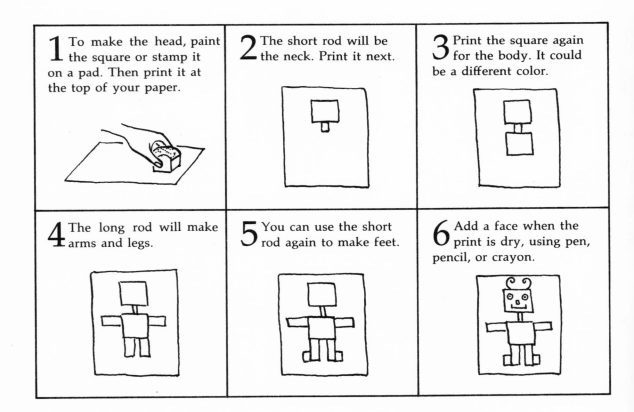

1 To make the head, paint the square or stamp it on a pad. Then print it at the top of your paper.

2 The short rod will be the neck. Print it next.

3 Print the square again for the body. It could be a different color.

4 The long rod will make arms and legs.

5 You can use the short rod again to make feet.

6 Add a face when the print is dry, using pen, pencil, or crayon.

Patterns, Letters, Butterflies, Flowers

Here are some more things to make with geometric blocks (see page 20).

You can create an interesting pattern using just one block. With one long rod and one short rod you can make all the letters of the alphabet. With rods and triangles you can make butterflies and flowers. These can be repeated to make more complicated patterns (see page 54).

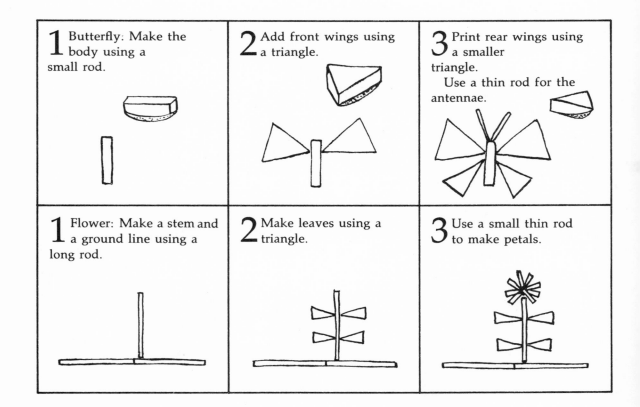

1 Butterfly: Make the body using a small rod.

2 Add front wings using a triangle.

3 Print rear wings using a smaller triangle.
   Use a thin rod for the antennae.

1 Flower: Make a stem and a ground line using a long rod.

2 Make leaves using a triangle.

3 Use a small thin rod to make petals.

PRINTMAKING

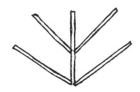

1 Another flower: Make a flower stem and leaf stems using a thin rod.

2 Use a small triangle to print leaves.

3 Add flower petals using another small triangle.

Buildings and Overprinting

You can make buildings in many shapes and styles using geometric blocks. After you have printed the basic building shape, you can print doors, windows, and other details on top of your first print. Printing on top of something already printed is called "overprinting."

Overprinting is usually used to add another color to a print. If you want the colors to blend, overprint while the first print is still wet. If you want them to look distinct, wait until the first color is dry before printing the second on top. You can overprint on top of overprinting with still more colors if you like.

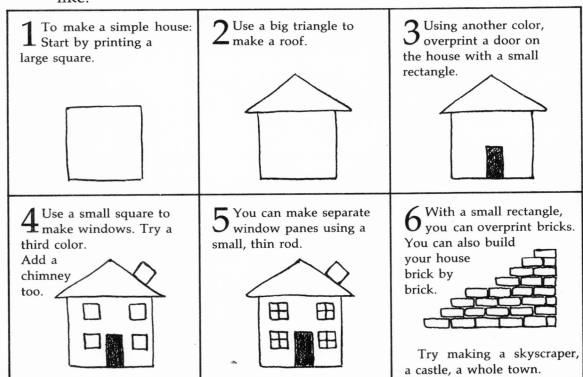

1 To make a simple house: Start by printing a large square.

2 Use a big triangle to make a roof.

3 Using another color, overprint a door on the house with a small rectangle.

4 Use a small square to make windows. Try a third color. Add a chimney too.

5 You can make separate window panes using a small, thin rod.

6 With a small rectangle, you can overprint bricks. You can also build your house brick by brick.

Try making a skyscraper, a castle, a whole town.

Potato Animals

Use geometric blocks to make a potato zoo. Overprint spots, stripes, eyes, and whiskers. Make your animals sit, stand, walk, run, and do other things.

1 Giraffe: Use a square to make a body.

2 Use a rod for the legs, neck, and head.

3 Add a tail and horns with a small rod. Overprint some spots and an eye.

1 Chicken: Make the body by printing a large circle. Use a small circle for the head.

2 Make the beak, wing, and tail with a small triangle. Overprint an eye with a tiny circle.

3 Print a short rod for legs. Use a very short rod for feet and comb.

1 Horse: Use a large rectangle for the body, a small one for the neck and head.

2 Use a long rod to print the legs and tail.

3 Use a small rod to make a mane and ears. Overprint an eye.

Potato Trees

There are many different ways to print trees using geometric blocks. Try making some unusual ones.

1 Use a triangle to make an evergreen tree.

2 Add a small rectangle for the trunk.

3 Overprint with small circles of different colors to make a Christmas tree.

Make some cards.

1 Print a long rectangle to make a tree trunk.

2 Make branches using rods.

3 Use small triangles, diamonds, squares, or circles to print leaves— green for summer, red, yellow, or orange for fall.

1 Make an apple or orange tree by printing small circles for fruit among the leaf shapes.

2 Or make a tree like this using long and short rods. Create new kinds of trees with unusual leaves.

3 Plant a forest using a repeat pattern (see p. 54).

Trucks and Trains

Print circles under square or rectangular blocks to make trucks, trains, buses, or cars.

Make airplanes, helicopters, and rocket ships. Invent some crazy vehicles of your own.

1 To make a pickup truck, print a rectangle for the cab and print again for the back.

2 Add a square for the engine.

3 Use circles to print wheels. Overprint a small rectangle for the window, and small circles for hubcaps.

1 To make a train engine, start with two rectangles.

2 Use a triangle for a funnel and a cowcatcher, small rectangles for a whistle and a sand dome. Overprint a window using a square.

3 Print circle wheels. Use black paint on the same circle to make smoke puffs. For gray smoke, print without adding more paint.

1 For a caboose, print a rectangle.

2 Use circles to make wheels. Add a small rectangle for the "cupola." Overprint with a small rectangle to make windows.

3 To make the track, use a long thin rod for rails. A tiny square makes the ties.

Other Shapes for Blocks

If you have a set of cooky cutters, you can use them to cut *nongeometric* printing blocks.

You can also cut your blocks out with a knife, making whatever shapes you like. First draw the outline of your shape on the potato with paint or ink and a small brush (pencil lines don't show up well on potatoes). You can erase by washing and drying the potato.

You will need: *a potato • a sharp knife • cooky cutters • newspaper • paint and brush or an ink pad • paper*

1 On a folded newspaper or cutting board, cut a thick slice (¾ inch, or 2 cm) from the middle of a large potato. Careful of your fingers!

2 Place the slice on the newspaper or board. Press a cooky cutter right through it.

Remove the potato shape from the cutter.

3 Now print your shape on paper. Add any decorations by overprinting or with pen or crayon when the print is dry. You can also print the outer part of the potato slice.

1 Cut a thick slice of potato. Paint the outline of your shape on the slice.

2 Hold the potato still with one hand. Cut around the shape with a sharp knife, being careful to keep your fingers out of the way.

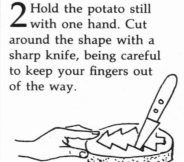

3 It may be easier to cut sections of the potato away as you go around your outline. You can also print the pieces you have cut off.

Relief Prints

By scratching or cutting lines into a smoothly cut piece of potato you can make another kind of potato printing block. When you print this kind of block, the scratched or cut lines on the potato will show up white on the paper. Only the raised parts around the lines will touch the paper and print color. A print made from areas or lines that are raised up from—in "relief" to—the rest of the surface is called a relief print.

A food coloring or ink stamp pad works well for these prints. Thick paint is more likely to get stuck in the lines, where it isn't wanted. You can make multicolored designs by painting parts of the potato with different colors. The lines will keep the colors separate.

You will need: *a cut potato • a pencil with a sharp point, a nail, toothpick, or other tool • newspaper • paint and a paint brush or stamp pad • paper to print on*

1 Scratch lines into the cut surface of a potato. Use a pencil, nail, or toothpick. Carefully scrape all bits of potato out of the lines and off the potato.

2 To make wide lines, use the end of a potato peeler or the head of a nail.

3 You can also use cooky cutters. Press the cutter about ¼ inch (1 cm) into the potato, then lift out. Using a nail or other tool, widen the lines made by the cutter.

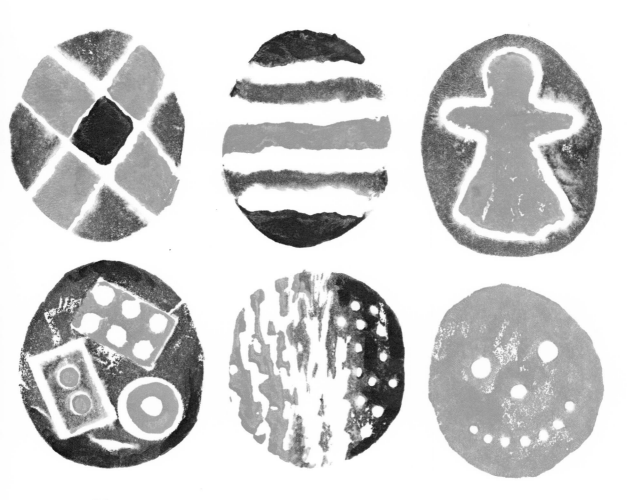

You can slice off the scratched part of the potato when you have finished printing from it and reuse the potato for another print. You can also slice off mistakes.

4 Try textures. Rub the potato over a food grater. Or hammer Lego blocks or other objects into a potato slice to leave their mark.

5 Use a pencil point or big nail to make a texture pattern, or to add eyes or other details. Jab the pencil or nail into the potato, twist, then lift out.

6 If you use thick paint for these prints, the pressure of printing may squeeze paint into lines and marks. Print with less pressure, widen the lines, or leave a little unpainted space around them.

Owls and Ghosts

Here are two easy projects using the relief print method. Draw your design on the cut surface of the potato before you scratch the lines in. Remember that pencil lines will not show up well on a cut potato; use a small paintbrush dipped in paint or ink. If you make a mistake in your drawing, you can erase it by wiping with a damp paper towel. Or wash and dry the potato and start over.

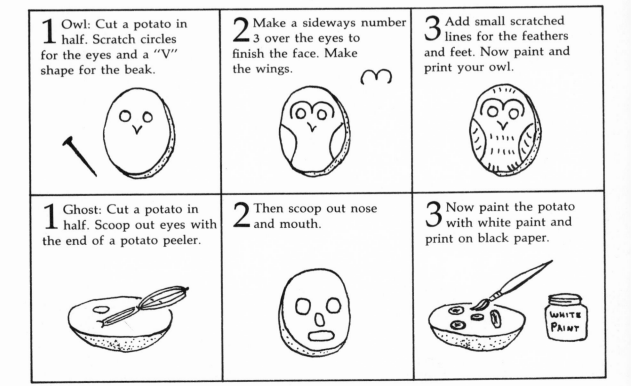

1 Owl: Cut a potato in half. Scratch circles for the eyes and a "V" shape for the beak.

2 Make a sideways number 3 over the eyes to finish the face. Make the wings.

3 Add small scratched lines for the feathers and feet. Now paint and print your owl.

1 Ghost: Cut a potato in half. Scoop out eyes with the end of a potato peeler.

2 Then scoop out nose and mouth.

3 Now paint the potato with white paint and print on black paper.

WHITE PAINT

Reversal

When you print your potato blocks, you will notice that pictures and lettering appear backward. What was on the left on the block is on the right on the print, and what was on the right is now on the left. This is called reversal.

The same thing happens when you look in the mirror. What you see in the mirror is like a print—it is reversed, with left and right sides changed around. If you want to know how something will look reversed, look at it in a mirror. Or you can draw on a piece of tracing paper and then turn the paper over. The drawing will show through from the other side, and will be reversed.

In printmaking, it may not matter that your picture comes out reversed. Sometimes, however, it does matter—when you are printing letters, for instance. You can get your drawing or letters to print the right way by planning for reversal when you make your block.

1 To print letters the right way around, write the word on paper. Hold the paper up to a mirror. Copy the mirror letters on the potato with paint or ink.

2 Or paint the word on one half of a cut potato. Make a monoprint (see p. 18) on the other half of the potato. Now you can scratch the letters, then print.

3 Make an alphabet on small squares. Typewriter letters are made like this, so is the type used for printing certain books.

Making Proofs

When you print a block for the first time to see what it will look like, that first print is called a "proof." The proof will show you if lines need to be widened or deepened. You may want to add more lines. After you have made any changes try another proof. You can also use proofs to see whether you need more or less paint or ink and to try out different papers or colors.

If you print a number of copies that are all colored just alike, using the same block, you have printed an "edition." Artists sign each print in an edition and number them in the order they were made.

1 Scratch or cut a picture in the center of your block. Remember, if you want something to face right in your print, you must make it face left on your potato.

2 Paint the picture one color, the background another.
Test results with a proof, then print and sign an edition.
Print a second edition using different colors.

3 Another way to print: Lay a piece of paper on top of the potato. Gently rub the back of the paper without wiggling it. Do not press into scratched lines. Peel the paper off.

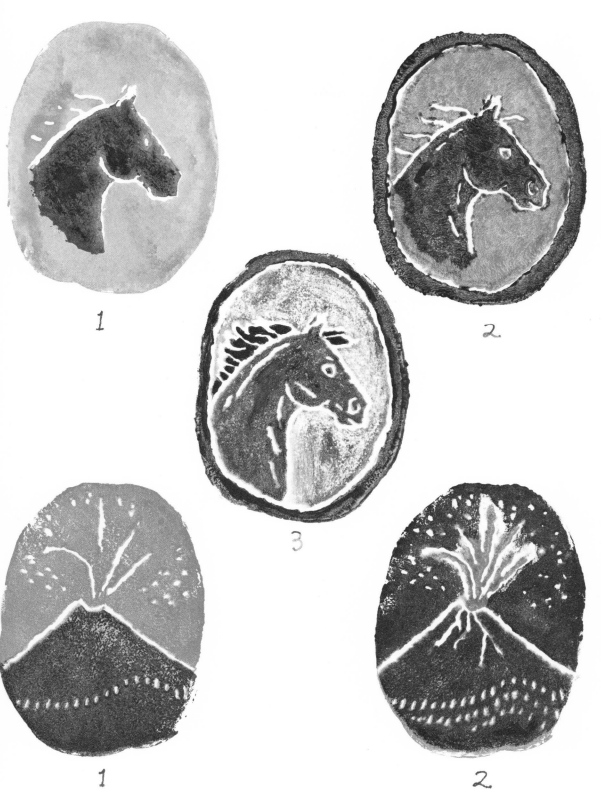

1

2

3

1

2

Filled-Line Prints

Relief blocks can be used another way. You can fill scratched or cut lines with paint or printing ink (special ink made for printing linoleum or wood blocks). Now the lines will show up on your print in color instead of as white spaces. Look at the prints on page 43 and then at the prints on page 45. They are made with the same blocks, but on page 43 only the raised parts of the potato were painted; on page 45 the lines were filled. Filled-line prints are trickier to print than relief prints, but they are fun to try.

1 Use a sharp knife to smoothly cut a thick slice of potato, about ½ inch or 1½ cm. (If you want to draw your design first, use a brush and paint or ink.)	**2** Cut shallow lines into the slice using a nail, sharp pencil point, or toothpick. The lines should be about $\frac{1}{16}$ to $\frac{1}{8}$ inch or 1 to 3 mm deep. 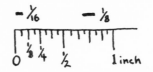	**3** Make sure that your lines are cleared of little bits of potato by running your tool through them. Wash bits off under running water.
4 Use thick poster paint, tempera, or printing inks. You can spread paint or printing ink on the potato with a knife. 	**5** Next, carefully wipe or scrape the paint or ink off the surface of the potato. Use the edge of a knife or a damp paper towel. Leave the lines full.	**6** You can also just spot-wipe, dabbing a small piece of damp towel between the lines. Remaining paint or ink will make a nice background. 

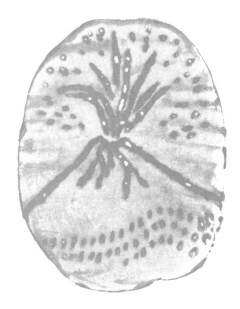

7 Now press the painted or inked side of the potato on a piece of paper.
Press the potato down very firmly, but be careful not to move it around.

8 Lift straight up and you have your first proof.
If it is blurry, your paint was probably too watery. Stir a little cornstarch into poster or tempera paint to thicken it.

9 If you are getting white lines instead of colored ones, the lines may be too deep, or there may not be enough paint or ink in them, or you may need to press harder on the potato.
A mixture of white and colored lines can look nice, however.

More on Filled-Line Prints

Potato prints made with paint- or ink-filled lines are a simple example of what are known as etchings and engravings. Artists' etchings and engravings are printed from flat pieces of metal called plates. Engravings can also be made on wood.

The difference between an etching and an engraving is the method used to make the lines on the plate. They are both printed in a similar way. First, ink is spread over the plate. Then it is wiped off the surface, leaving the lines filled. A heavy piece of machinery called a printing press presses the plate hard against the paper to force the ink out and make a print.

In making a potato etching or engraving, the potato takes the place of the metal plate. The table or counter you are working on is like the bottom of the press and your hand is the top.

1 Make some fossils. Try a trilobite: On the potato slice scratch a half moon for the head.

2 Add a body with lines for the separate segments.

3 Now add legs and feelers. Print as shown on p. 44. (Or print as a relief print: see p. 36.)

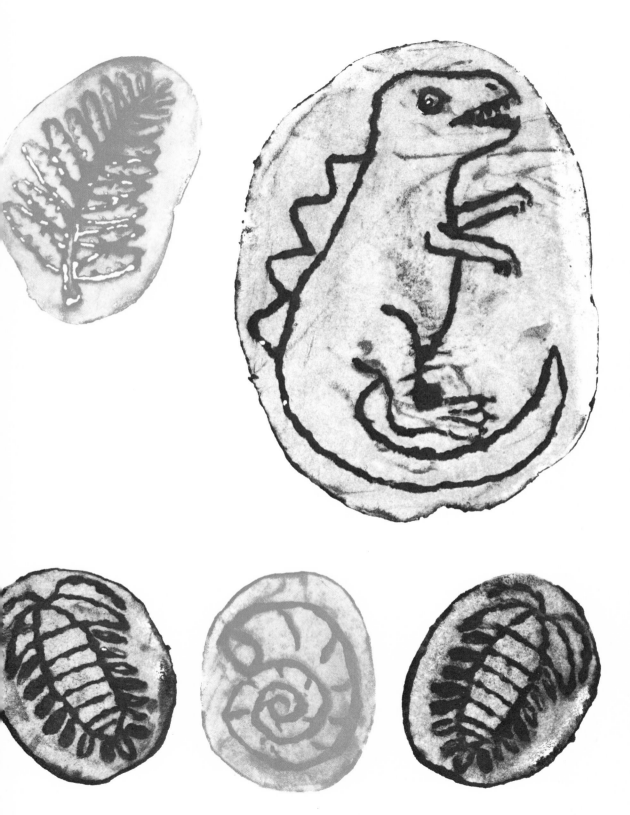

Carved Relief Prints

Another way to make relief prints from potatoes is to carve them by cutting with linoleum cutters or a knife. Cut lines will have smooth, straight edges. Scratched lines usually have rough edges. Prints made from carved blocks will look a lot like linocuts (prints made from carved linoleum blocks) or woodcuts (prints made from carved wood blocks).

The easiest tools to use for carving are lino cutters. (If you don't have lino cutters see the directions on page 52 for carving with a knife.) To make the block, you cut away—carve out—all surface areas that you do not want to show up in your print. The raised areas or lines which you leave will be printed.

Potatoes, because they are soft, are much easier to cut than linoleum or wood. This means that your cutters are less apt to slip out of control than if you were carving something harder. However, *always* keep the hand that is holding the potato out of the way of your cutters.

1 Linoleum cutters are made of three pieces.

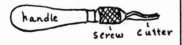

The cutter (the end part) fits into the screw, which is turned to tighten. Cutters come in different shapes and sizes.

2 To use, hold the cutter end at an angle to the potato and push.

Always keep the hand holding the potato behind the cutter.

3 Be sure to wash and dry the cutters after you use them, or they will get rusty and dull. Remove the cutter ends from the handle.

Using Linoleum Cutters

Basic directions for using a lino cutter are on page 48. To make your prints, you may also want to get a brayer (a roller for spreading ink), some water-base printing ink, and some rice paper.

1 For these prints, be sure to cut the potato in half smoothly. Use a sharp knife. If the surface is uneven or rough some lines may not print well.

Plan your design. You can draw it on the potato with paint or ink.

2 Using a V-shaped cutter cut a trench around areas you want to print. Clear away scraps of potato as you go.

3 Cut trenches so that the edges slope away from the parts you will print.

Undercut lines are apt to bend or break.

4 You can also use V-shaped cutters to create textures and details.

5 Use larger cutters to scoop out thick lines or areas.

6 Try a proof to see if you need to cut away more potato.

7 If ridges are printing in what should be a white area, scoop them off.

Trim the edges, unless you want a frame around your picture.

8 With a brayer, spread water-base printing ink on a cooky sheet. Roll ink onto the potato with the brayer, or stamp the potato into the spread-out ink.

9 When you print, try putting the paper on top of the potato as shown on p. 42. This is how linocuts and woodcuts are usually printed without a printing press.

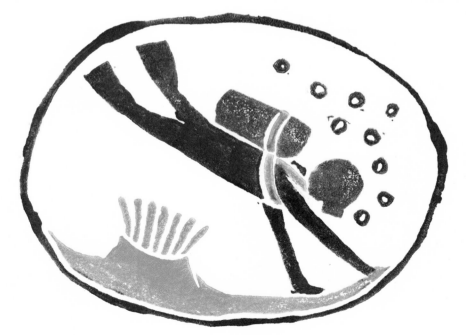

Carving with a Knife

You can use a knife instead of lino cutters to make a carved relief print. You can also try a knife for some of the cuts, and lino cutters for others on the same block.

1 Cut the potato smoothly in half. Draw your design. If your drawing does not come to the edges of the potato, cut off the edge pieces, leaving a small margin.

2 With the point of your knife, carefully outline your drawing. Cut about ⅛ to ¼ inch (3–5 mm) deep. Be careful not to undercut.

3 For areas near the edge of the block, cut in from the edge to meet the outline cut.

Be careful not to cut the hand holding the potato.

4 To cut out areas in the middle of the block, make a cut at an angle to your outline cut. This leaves a small trench.

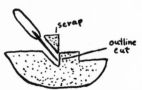

5 Use the end of a potato peeler to scoop out areas between trenches. Or cut out by making more trenches.

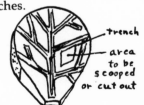

6 For narrow lines, cut V-shaped trenches on both sides of the line. Very fine lines are hard to make and often will not last for many prints.

7 To make lines within a solid area, it may be easier to scratch them in, as shown on p. 36.

8 When you print you can leave scratched lines to print white or fill them with a color (see p. 44). Wipe off extra paint or ink. Use another color for the raised areas.

9 A nail or other sharp point can be used to notch edges of raised areas.

Combining Blocks

A design or picture can be built up from several separate parts. You can make a carved block for each part. Then print the blocks so that the parts of the design join together.

You can also use several different blocks to make prints that look like stencil designs.

When a design is made by printing the same block or combination of blocks repeatedly, this design is called a repeat pattern. Fabric and wallpaper are often printed using repeat patterns.

1 Carve a block with a flower on it.

2 Next, cut a block with a stem and leaves. Make sure the top of the stem comes to the edge of the block.

3 Now print the flower using a bright color. Then print the stem and leaves below the flower.
  Repeat for a row of flowers.

1 For repeat patterns, simple blocks, such as the stencil design blocks shown here, work well.

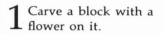

2 Print the blocks one on top of another. Or alternate blocks and colors.

3 You can also make repeat patterns using any other blocks you have made. Turn blocks upside down or sideways. Experiment.

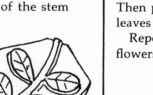

1 Another flower: Cut a single petal on a block. When you print you can overlap the petals to make the flower fuller.

2 Cut a block for the stem (or use a thin rod— you can bend a thin rod for a curved stem).

Make a block for a single leaf.

3 Now print the flower, stem, and leaves.

Fabric Printing

You can also use potato printing blocks to print on fabric. If you want to be able to wash the printed fabric, you must use permanent paint or ink. Acrylic paint and textile screen printing ink (sold in art stores and in art departments in chain stores) are your best choices.

Acrylic paint, which comes in tubes, can be thinned with water and cleaned up with soap and water before it dries. Once it is dry it will not wash off, and acrylic printed fabric may be machine washed and dried.

Textile screen printing ink comes in cans. These inks can also be thinned with water. Clean up with soap and water before the ink dries. Screen printing ink must be heat treated to make it permanent. See the directions on page 57.

All fabric that is to be washed later should be washed before printing.

Print a T-shirt, wall hanging, or throw pillow cover. Try some repeat patterns as shown on page 54.

---

1 Make sure your fabric is not wrinkled. Iron if needed. Fabric may be thumbtacked or stapled around heavy cardboard to keep it smooth and still.

2 Acrylic paint may be rolled out with a brayer, thinned with a little water, and applied with a paint brush, or thinned and spread out on damp paper towels to make a stamp pad.

3 For clear, crisp prints, print on smooth, dry fabric. If you want the print to "bleed" so that some of the paint will spread into the background, dampen the fabric, then print.

Test on sample pieces of fabric.

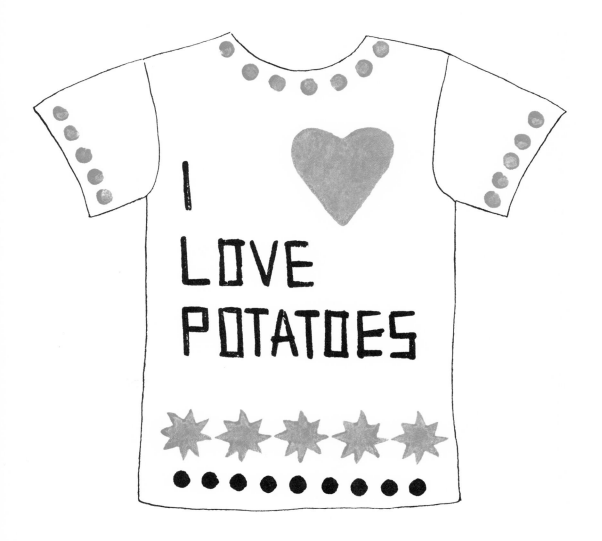

I ♥ LOVE POTATOES

4 When using textile screen printing ink: Choose a fabric that can be ironed or machine dried. The ink can be worked with in the same ways as acrylic paint. After the fabric has been printed, allow it to dry, about 20–30 minutes.

5 To permanently "set" the ink: Use a dry medium-hot iron. Place a clean piece of fabric between the iron and the print. Iron 2–3 minutes.

6 Or: Put the printed dry fabric in a clothes drier set on "hot" and tumble for 45 minutes.

Large Designs

Large designs or pictures can also be made by combining differ-ent kinds of potato printing blocks. You can use carved blocks in combination with geometric or scratched line blocks. These prints often look as though they were made from a single potato block, but they can be bigger than even the biggest potatoes.

1 To make a large tree, first print a trunk, using a rod or rods. Scratch lines for the bark.

2 Next print a carved block of a small tree to make branches for your large tree.

3 Add smaller branches using another carved block. Next make a block with a leaf carved on it.

1 Thanksgiving turkey: Start with a potato cut in half for the body. Scratch lines for feathers. Add legs and feet using a long and a short rod.

2 Next cut a block shaped like a 2 for the head and neck. Overprint the wattle and an eye using small pieces of potato.

3 Now cut a block shaped like a feather. Scratch or cut lines into it. Print it to make the tail.

Creating Backgrounds

You can use one type of potato print as a background for another. To make a simple oval frame background for a carved block, print an oval-shaped potato half using one color, then overprint with the carved block in another color. Use a round potato half for a round frame, or trim edges to make a square.

When making a large picture combining several blocks, any simple block can be printed repeatedly to create a background. You may want to use a light color or dilute your paint if you are going to print a darker color on top. Overlap the same form until your piece of paper, or the part you want, is covered. Then print a carved block or other potato block on top. If you vary the tone of your background color from light to dark, it will give the print the appearance of depth and texture. You can also make backgrounds with a textured look by using a scratched or carved block.

1 To make a landscape, start with the sky. Use a potato cut in half, a simple geometric block, or a textured block.

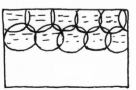

2 Now print hills using a quarter of a potato or a triangle-shaped block. Make a field, using a carved block or a rod.

3 Print trees made from carved or geometric blocks. Add a barn and a horse.

Moonscape

Space
black paper   p. 16

Moon background
a half potato
relief print marked with a nail   p. 36
overprinted   p. 26

Crater
scratched block with filled lines   p. 44

Moon buggy
geometric blocks   p. 20
overprinted   p. 26

Astronaut
carved relief block   p. 48
reversal planned for   p. 40

Small planet
geometric block   p. 20
mixed inks on stamp pad   p. 12

Planet with rings
carved relief block   p. 48
monoprinted   p. 18

Stars
cut blocks   p. 34

Star nebula
scraps   p. 20
printed from dark to light   p. 14

Rocket ship
geometric blocks   p. 20
overprinted   p. 26

Index

Animals
  butterflies, 24,25
  chickens, 28,29
  fish, 49,50,51
  giraffes, 28,29
  horses, 28,29,42,43,45,61
  monkeys, 4
  owls, 38,39
  rabbits, 11
  seals, 2
  turkeys, 58,59
  wolves, 52,53
Backgrounds, 60,61
Boats, 13,51
Brayer, *see* tools
Buildings, 26,27
Cooky Cutters, *see* tools
Diver, 51
Editions, 42
Engravings, 46
Etchings, 46
Fabric, printing on, 54,56,57
Filled lines, 44,45,46,47
Flowers, 24,25,54,55
Food coloring, 12,13
Fossils, 46,47
  dinosaur, 47
  trilobite, 46,47
Ghosts, 38,39
Helicopters, 33
Ink
  drawing, 12,13
  textile screen printing, 56,57
  printing, 44,45,50
Landscapes, 60,61
Letters, 24,25,40,41
Linoleum cutters, *see* tools
Monoprints, 18,19

Moonscape, 62
Overprinting, 26,27
Paints
  for printing, 10,56,57
  to thicken, 45
  to thin, 14,56,57
Papers for printing, 16,17,50
Patterns
  repeat, 24,30,37,54,55
  stencil, 54,55
Pinwheels, 14,15
Potatoes
  selecting, 8
  storing, 8
Printing blocks
  combined, 54,55,58,59,60,61
  geometric, 20,21
  nongeometric, 34,35
Printing press, 46,50
Proofs, 42
Relief print, 36,37,38,39,44,45,46,47
  carved, 48,49,50,51,52,53
Reversal, 18,40,41
Robots, 22,23
Scratched lines, 36,37
Snowmen, 16,17
Stamp pads, 12,13,14,36
Sun, 13
Tools
  brayer, 50,56
  cooky cutters, 34,35,36
  kitchen tools, 8,9,21,37
  linoleum cutter, 48,50
Trains, 32,33
Trees, 30,31,34,35,52,58,59
Trucks, 32,33
Volcano, 43,45
Waves, 13